I dedicate this book

to the loving and loyal followers of Camper and Leo.

It warms my heart to know that you enjoy them as much as we do!

Camper and Leo were an unlikely pair

But there was something they both could share.

Going on adventures was their favorite thing to do.

They always loved to play in the sun and snow too.

amper was an English Lab with soft, white fur upon his back.

He was always ready for a snack.

Camper liked to snuggle and play with toys

And spending time with his family brought him joy.

Leo was a Maine Coon cat.

He was huge, even when he sat!

His fur was always soft to touch

And he loved his family very much.

Most people think cats and dogs do not get along.

But Camper and Leo could prove them all wrong.

The boys loved to play together

Especially in winter weather.

One snowy day, as dad pulled Leo in a sled

Camper followed where he led.

Everyone was having a wonderful time

Enjoying the snow. It was sublime!

Dad had to stop to button his coat.

Camper had a thought and grabbed the rope.

He began pulling the sled this way and that

While Leo watched and calmly sat.

As Camper pulled the sled away,

Leo knew he could jump but decided to stay.

On the sled he thought it was nice

Being pulled by his friend on the snow and ice.

All around the yard they went

Until their energy had been spent.

It was more fun than anything they had done before.

Leo and Camper could not wait to do more!

The two best friends then strolled inside.

They sat by the fire as their wet fur dried.

Leo and Camper snuggled up close.

They could not quite decide who'd had fun the most.

As they laid down for a nap,

Leo cozied up to Camper's lap.

They thought of the things that they could do,

More adventures to come for these two.